W9-ASL-513

EYEWITNESS
CHICAGO

EYEWITNESS
CHICAGO

Written by
JUDY SUTTON TAYLOR

Consultant for Chicago Public Schools
JOHN DUDLEY

Chicago Bears helmet

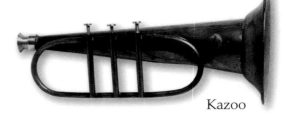

Kazoo

Louis Armstrong album cover

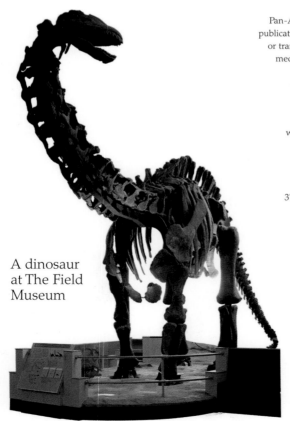

A dinosaur at The Field Museum

Route 66 sign

DK

LONDON, NEW YORK,
MELBOURNE, MUNICH, AND DELHI

Senior editors Ros Walford, Michele Wells
Senior art editor Ann Cannings
Senior DTP designer David McDonald
Senior production controller Sarah Hughes
Picture researchers Myriam Mégharbi,
Evi Peroulaki, Karen VanRoss
Cartographer John Plumer
Proofreader Deborah Lock
Indexer Hilary Bird
Associate publisher Nigel Duffield

First published in the United States in 2011
by DK Publishing, 375 Hudson Street, New York, New York 10014

10 9 8 7 6 5 4 3 2 1
001-182278-Sep/11

Copyright © 2011 Dorling Kindersley Limited

DK books are available at special discounts
when purchased in bulk for sales promotions,
premiums, fundraising, or educational use.

For details, contact:
DK Publishing Special Markets
375 Hudson Street, New York, New York 10014
SpecialSales@dk.com

A catalog record for this book is available
from the Library of Congress.

ISBN: 978-0-7566-8872-1

Color reproduction by
Media Development & Printing Ltd,
United Kingdom.

Printed and bound by
Hung Hing, China.

Discover more at
www.dk.com

Banner for
Chicago Botanic Garden

AUTHOR
Judy Sutton Taylor is the editor of *Time
Out Chicago Kids*, a bimonthly arts and
entertainment magazine for Chicago area
families. She acted as lead editor of *Time Out
Chicago 2008 Eating and Drinking Guide*, which
featured articles and information on more
than 1,500 Chicago bars and restaurants.
She has appeared on ABC-7 news segments,
discussing trends, new products, and things
to do around Chicago.

CONSULTANT FOR CHICAGO PUBLIC SCHOOLS
John Dudley is a National Board Certified
history teacher. He has been involved in
education since 1997. John has worked with
the Chicago Public Schools as a classroom
teacher since 2000. He is currently teaching
a variety of social studies courses at the
Collins Academy in the North Lawndale
neighborhood. John currently lives in Chicago's
East Village neighborhood with his wife, Nora.

Contents

A gargoyle at
the University
of Chicago

6
What is Chicago?

8
Chicagoland

10
Early history

12
Lakes and rivers

14
The first Chicagoans

16
The founding of Chicago

18
The railroads

20
Waterways

22
Industrial boom

24
The Great Chicago Fire

26
Rebuilding the city

28
The Chicago World's Fair

30
Political change

32
The Jazz Age

34
Multicultural Chicago

36
Skyscrapers

38
Transportation

40
Banking boom

42
Great museums

44
University of Chicago

46
Sports

48
Entertainment

50
The media

52
Famous food

54
Events and attractions

56
Green city

58
Famous Chicagoans

60
Questions and answers

62
Fascinating facts

63
Glossary

64
Index

What is Chicago?

CHICAGO IS IN THE MIDWESTERN United States. It is so many things to so many people. The city motto is *urbs en horto*, which means "city in a garden." It has beautiful parks, lots of trees, and a lovely lakefront. It has world-class museums, art, and music. It is one of the busiest transportation centers in the country. It is also a center of big business. Most of all, Chicago is always exciting.

Chicago flag

The white stripes are for the North, West, and South sides of the city. The blue stripes represent Lake Michigan, the Chicago River, and the Illinois and Michigan Canal. The stars are for Fort Dearborn (see p16), the Great Chicago Fire (see pp24-5), and the two World's Fairs (see pp28-9) held here in 1893 and 1933.

KEY

■ Illinois

See p9 for a map of this area

GREATER CHICAGO

- Highway
- Major road
- Local road
- Main railroad
- Minor railroad
- State line
- Urban area

0 miles 10

Chicago jazz

The 1920s were the height of the Jazz Age in Chicago. Many black musicians from the South moved to Chicago to perform. The most famous was a trumpet player named Louis Armstrong (above). There were many jazz clubs on the South Side. A few are still around today.

The Windy City

Chicago has a few nicknames, but "Windy City" is the one that's the most popular. Some people think it's because of the windy weather here. Others say the nickname came from politicians and locals being full of hot air, or nonsense.

Meatpacking industry

Chicago was the largest meatpacking city in the country from the Civil War until the 1920s. Lots of farmers here raised livestock. The many railroads made it easy to transport meat from here to the rest of the country. Around this time, Chicago got the nickname "Hog Butcher to the World."

Transportation hub

A trip across the US often includes a stop in Chicago. The city's location in the center of the country makes it a hub, or center point, for all kinds of travel and business.

Route 66 is a highway that starts in Chicago and travels west to Santa Monica, California.

Midwest metropolis

Almost 10 million people live in the Chicago area. It is the biggest midpoint between the East and West coasts. It's the third-largest city in the US. People live and work in the tall skyscrapers, and many big businesses have offices here.

Chicagoland

CHICAGO IS A CITY OF NEIGHBORHOODS.
These neighborhoods are in parts of the city known as the North Side, South Side, and West Side. (Lake Michigan is Chicago's "East Side.") Many of the neighborhoods in the city center are home to famous museums, buildings, and parks. Some of the suburbs also have fun places to visit. The people who live here call the city and suburbs "Chicagoland."

Two bronze lions guard the entrance of the Art Institute of Chicago.

World-class museums

There are many famous museums in Chicago (see pp42–3). The Field Museum of Natural History has Sue, one of the largest T. rex fossils in the world. You can learn about stars and planets at the Adler Planetarium. The Art Institute of Chicago has paintings by Picasso, Monet, and other famous artists.

Skyscrapers

Some of the tallest buildings in the world are in Chicago (see pp36–7). The Willis Tower (above) is the tallest building in the United States. People can stand in a glass box at the top called "the Ledge." There are boat tours on the Chicago River that talk about all of Chicago's big buildings, too.

Parks and gardens

Chicago thinks of itself as a "green" city. There are about 570 city parks here. There are also rooftop gardens on many buildings, including City Hall (see p56). Millennium Park is a large park in downtown Chicago. It has a garden, ice-skating rink, concert space, and public art.

Animal attractions

There are two big zoos in the Chicago area. Lincoln Park Zoo is one of the oldest zoos in the United States. It is free to get in. They have 1,200 animals, a farm, and a carousel. Brookfield Zoo is west of the city. It has a butterfly garden and a large space for bears to roam. The Shedd Aquarium (see p42) holds more than 5 million gallons of water. Dolphins, whales, penguins, and 25,000 fish live here.

Map of central Chicago

The streets of Chicago are laid out in a grid. The center of the city is the downtown business district. It is called the Loop. Lake Michigan lies to the east. Neighborhoods fan out from the Loop to the north, south, and west.

Fun and games

Navy Pier is a great place for families to visit. It has an amusement park with a 150-foot Ferris wheel. There is also a children's museum and an IMAX theater. People often take boat rides on Lake Michigan that leave from here.

A sports-minded city

Chicagoans love sports. Baseball fans who live on the South Side like the White Sox. The ones who live on the North Side like the Cubs. Chicago's other big sports teams are the Bears (football), Bulls (basketball), and Blackhawks (hockey). The Race to Mackinac is a famous sailboat race that starts in Chicago and goes to Michigan every July. Runners race in the Chicago Marathon every October.

CENTRAL CHICAGO
- Chicago attractions
- Railroad station
- Parks
- Highway
- Railroad

0　　　　yards 1000

LINCOLN PARK

Lincoln Park Zoo

OLD TOWN

Lincoln Park

West North Avenue

GOLD COAST

RIVER NORTH

West Division Street

West Chicago Avenue

RUSH AND DIVISION

STREETERVILLE

Magnificent Mile

East Grand Avenue

Navy Pier

Chicago River

East Wacker Drive

West Wacker Drive

LOOP

Ogilvie Transportation Center

City Hall

Millennium Park

E Randolph St

West Madison Street

Union Station

Willis Tower

Art Institute of Chicago

West Jackson Boulevard

Monroe Harbor

WEST LOOP

LaSalle Street Station

West Congress Parkway

Van Buren Street Station

Chicago Harbor

Grant Park

PRINTERS ROW

Lake Michigan

West Roosevelt Road

Shedd Aquarium

Adler Planetarium

Field Museum

Burnham Park Harbor

Dan Ryan Expressway

South Halsted Street

North Halsted Street

North Clark Street

North Lake Shore Drive

Lake Michigan

South Lake Shore Drive

Northerly Island Park

PILSEN

SOUTH LOOP

West Cermak Road

Dan Ryan Expressway

Stevenson Expressway

HYDE PARK 3 miles

Early history

FOR MILLIONS OF YEARS, Chicago was covered only by ice. This period was called the Ice Age. About 20,000 years ago, the Ice Age ended. The Earth started to get warmer and the ice began to move. It left behind water, clay, gravel, and sand. They were filled with minerals. Soon, land formed and forests grew. Large animals came here to eat the grass and plants. Indian tribes followed the animals.

Bison

Bison are also called American buffalo. Huge herds of them came to this area to roam and graze. They liked to eat the short grass on the prairies. Elk and deer also came here to eat. You can still find these animals in the Midwest today, but in much smaller numbers.

Mammals

Large mammals were the first residents here. Two kinds were mammoths and mastodons. They both looked a lot like elephants and were about the same size. Indians hunted them for food and clothing. The last of these animals died about 10,000 years ago. They are now extinct.

Mammoth

Mammoths had curved tusks that were anywhere from three to 16 feet long.

Mastodon

The Ice Age

Between 14,000 and 20,000 years ago, the glaciers that covered the Great Lakes region started to move. They carved out big holes in the earth. As the glaciers melted, the holes filled with water (like the ones shown above). These became the Great Lakes. A big lake was formed called Lake Chicago. It dried up and left behind a smaller lake now called Lake Michigan.

Prairie landcape

When the Ice Age ended, trees such as maples and oaks grew in the Midwest. They formed forests. But the climate was very dry. There wasn't enough water for these trees. They were replaced by prairies—large areas of grass and shrubs. The Indians liked that the prairies attracted a lot of animals. They burned prairie fires to stop the forests from growing again.

Glaciers

Glaciers are large sheets of ice. Sometimes when they move, they carve out big valleys, as shown in the picture below. Other times they make the ground very flat. This type of glacier once covered the Midwest. That is why the land is so flat here today. When the glaciers moved, they left behind piles of soil and rocks. These piles are called moraines and can look like big hills.

Lakes and rivers

THE LAKES AND RIVERS AROUND Chicago are what first made the city important. Travel and trading between points to the north and south had to come through Chicago. It was the fastest and easiest way to get to other parts of North America. At first, travelers had to cross the Chicago Portage, a short land route that connected Lake Michigan with the rivers that flow to the Mississippi River. Later, a canal was built to make travel easier.

Great Lakes

There are five Great Lakes. Their names are Michigan, Superior, Huron, Ontario, and Erie. They lie at the border between the United States and Canada. They are the largest group of freshwater lakes in the world. They cover more than 94,000 square miles.

Great Lakes Basin (see map below)

Great Lakes Basin

When rain falls on high ground, it flows downhill in rivers and collects in lakes. The area where the rain flows from is called a "watershed." The Great Lakes Basin is the watershed for the Great Lakes.

Great Lakes Watershed

- Great Lakes Basin
- State boundary
- International boundary
- ○ City
- ○ Town

0   50   100   miles 150

CANADA

Thunder Bay

MINNESOTA

Lake Superior

Duluth

Sault Ste. Marie   Sudbury   North Bay

Minneapolis Saint Paul

WISCONSIN

Green Bay

Mississippi River

Milwaukee

IOWA

Des Moines

Davenport

Rockford

Chicago

South Bend

ILLINOIS

Illinois River

INDIANA

Lake Michigan

MICHIGAN

Grand Rapids

Lansing

Detroit

Toledo

OHIO

Lake Huron

Georgian Bay

Sarnia

Lake Erie

Cleveland

Erie

PENNSYLVANIA

Toronto

Burlington

Lake Ontario

Buffalo

Rochester

Syracuse

NEW YORK

New York

Peterborough

OTTAWA

Montréal

St Lawrence Seaway

N
W   E
S

UNITED STATES OF AMERICA

Bridges link streets over the Chicago River in the Loop.

Chicago River

Many early settlers chose to live in Chicago because of the Chicago River. It is one of the waterways that connect the Great Lakes to the Mississippi River. There are three parts to it: the North Branch, the South Branch, and the Main Stem.

Sand dunes

The glaciers from the Ice Age left behind lots of sand when they melted. Wind blew the sand over plants and rocks on the Lake Michigan shore. That is how sand dunes along the beaches were created. Some are as tall as 300 feet.

Lake Michigan

This is the third-largest of the Great Lakes. It is the only one entirely in the United States. (Parts of all the others are in Canada.) Chicago is the biggest city on Lake Michigan. There are many skyscrapers next to the city beaches.

Illinois River

The Illinois River also helps to link the Great Lakes with the Mississippi River. The Illinois and Michigan Canal (I & M) was built in 1848 to connect it to the Chicago River and to make travel easier.

The first Chicagoans

By the early 1600s, there were about 20,000 Native Americans living in the Great Lakes area. They came from different tribes, and traded and sometimes fought with each other. Many lived in Chicago during summer, then traveled to warmer places in winter. They grew corn, hunted, and fished here. When white settlers arrived, they wanted the tribes to give up the land. Many tried to fight the settlers, but lost and moved west.

Chief Keokuk
The Sauk Chief Keokuk tried to work peacefully with settlers who wanted Illinois land. His rival was Chief Black Hawk, who wanted to stay and fight. Instead, Keokuk moved his followers to land in Iowa.

Winnebago headdress
The Winnebago are also known as the Ho-Chunk tribe. They came from the Green Bay area in Wisconsin. Warriors from the tribe wore roach headdresses when they fought an enemy. These were made from dyed animal hair.

Potawatami pouches

Between the late 1700s and the 1830s, the Potawatomi were the biggest tribe in Chicago. Like other tribes, they signed treaties with white settlers and traded with them. They made deerskin tobacco pouches (left) and shoes.

Ojibwa sugar cones

The Ojibwa were a big tribe in the Great Lakes area. They and other tribes believed that land should be shared by everyone, like air and sunlight. They stored sugar in molds made from tree bark, such as these cones.

Silk ribbon sewn to cloth

Decorated with metal brooches

Sauk and Fox tribes

The Sauk and Fox were two tribes that combined into one. They were farming people who grew crops like squash, which could be dried for storage (above). In 1831, the government forced the tribes from Chicago. A small group led by Chief Black Hawk stayed to fight and many were killed.

Miami clothing

The Miami tribe was in Chicago in the late 1600s. They spoke the same language as the Illini tribe. They traded wool, ribbon, and beads with white settlers. Miami women used these items to decorate clothes, like this woolen skirt.

Fine beadwork

The founding of Chicago

BY THE 1600S, NATIVE AMERICANS HAD LIVED in the Midwest for hundreds of years. The first Europeans came here in the 1670s. They liked that Chicago was near the water and useful for shipping. Chicago stayed very small for the next 200 years. But once settlers came from the East and started businesses, it grew fast. Illinois became a state in 1818. The city of Chicago was founded in 1833.

Explorers and missionaries

In 1673 Jacques Marquette and Louis Joliet "discovered" Chicago. Marquette was a French missionary who came to convert Native Americans to Christianity. Joliet was a French explorer. Local tribes showed them an area they called "Chicago." It was a shortcut between the Mississippi River and the Great Lakes.

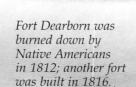

Fort Dearborn

Fort Dearborn was built on the Chicago River in 1803. It was made to protect white Americans from Native Americans. In 1812, the US had a war with the British who joined the Native Americans. The people who lived at Fort Dearborn left to find a safer place. They were attacked by Native Americans and many were killed. The attack was called the Fort Dearborn massacre.

Fort Dearborn was burned down by Native Americans in 1812; another fort was built in 1816.

La Salle

Robert Cavelier de La Salle was a French explorer. He explored the Great Lakes and Mississippi River. He "discovered" parts of Illinois in 1680. LaSalle Street is a large street in downtown Chicago that is named for him.

Sauk tribesmen like Black Hawk plucked all of their hair except for one section.

Chicago's first citizen

Jean Baptiste Point Du Sable was the first person to move to Chicago. He came here around 1782. He built a trading post on the Chicago River. He became rich by trading fur and other items with Native Americans and French settlers.

Chief Black Hawk

By the 1830s, more and more white settlers were moving here. In 1832, Chief Black Hawk led a group of Sauk Indians in a battle to keep their land. But most of his men died and they lost. The Treaty of Chicago was signed in 1833. The Sauk agreed to sell land in Illinois and Wisconsin to settlers. That was the year Chicago was founded.

Du Sable's farmhouse was said to be filled with expensive furniture.

The railroads

CHICAGO IS THE MOST important railroad center in North America. The first tracks were laid here in 1848 with lead from mines in northwestern Illinois. Soon, many more railroad lines were built. The trains moved grain, livestock, and other goods. They traveled east and west. Soon, people began taking train trips to and from Chicago.

Union Station

Chicago's major train station is Union Station. The current station was built in 1925. It replaced one that had been at the same site since 1881. In the late 1800s, there were several big train stations around Chicago's business district. Each served a different train line. The new Union Station was built to give the city one central train station.

All aboard!

The *Pioneer* was the first train to travel west from Chicago. On November 20, 1848, it rode along the newly built Galena & Chicago Union Railroad line. It took 100 people to Elmhurst, 8 miles from Chicago. The *Pioneer* returned with a load of wheat. You can see it today at the Chicago History Museum (see p43).

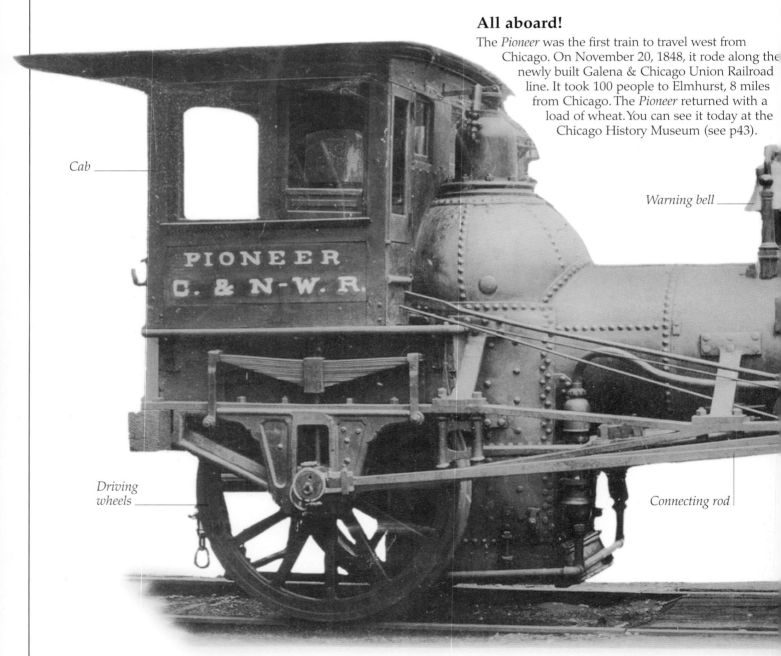

Cab

Warning bell

PIONEER
C. & N-W. R.

Driving wheels

Connecting rod

Pullman neighborhood

Neighborhoods were built near railroad lines for people who worked in the railroads. Pullman was one of these areas. There were small row homes for workers and large homes for wealthy families.

Train travel

In the late 1800s, many trains going across the United States stopped in Chicago. It was a good middle point between the East and West coasts. Posters advertising train travel were put up around the city.

Smokestack

Boiler

Chicago's Loop

Chicago grew as the railroads grew. In the city center there was a circle of tracks. Offices and warehouses were built nearby. They belonged to companies that used the trains to transport their goods. The area was named the Loop for the circle of tracks. Today, it is the central business district.

Pilot

Waterways

CHICAGO'S LOCATION NEAR lakes and rivers helped it become a big city, but man-made waterways made it bigger and better. The first underground sewers in the United States were made here. One canal changed the direction of the Chicago River to keep drinking water clean. Others let boats travel all the way from the Atlantic Ocean to the Gulf of Mexico through Chicago. Shipping became a big business. More ports were built to help meet new demands.

Early swing bridges
People needed to cross the Chicago river. Swing bridges were built that could let tall ships through. The first swing bridge was built at State Street in 1889. People stood on the bridge when it moved. It had no barriers. Sometimes people fell into the water.

Bridges today
Swing bridges were replaced with other types of bridge. Today, 20 drawbridges cross the Chicago River in the downtown area. The bridges are raised to let boats go past to and from Lake Michigan.

Sewers and water supply

Chicago often flooded because it was flat. In 1871, a sewer system was built to help stop the flooding. It was the first one in the US. Pipes were laid above ground and covered with soil. Streets and buildings had to be raised above the pipes by about 12 feet. Tunnels were also built to carry fresh water to the city. Today, there are 65 miles of water tunnels beneath Chicago.

Sanitary and Ship Canal

This canal was built in 1900 to replace the I & M Canal. The new canal was deeper and it used locks to change the flow of the Chicago River. This helped to send polluted water to the south instead of into Lake Michigan.

Illinois and Michigan Canal

The Illinois and Michigan Canal (I & M Canal) was built in 1848. It was built to connect the Illinois River to the Chicago River. It made an easy route from the Great Lakes to the Mississippi River. Chicago became the most important transportation center in the US.

Calumet Harbor

In the early 1900s, Chicago needed more ports for its growing shipping business. The ports were built on the South Side instead of downtown, so big barges could dock. The largest was Calumet Harbor. It is still an important port today.

Industrial boom

Goods used to just pass through Chicago. In the 1860s, things changed. Chicago became a city where goods were made. Food, clothing, and fuel were made here. So were many other things. People moved here to work and the city got bigger. But companies wanted to keep costs down. Many factories were unsafe and workers were not paid much money. Later, conditions got better. Some companies founded around that time are still in Chicago today.

Streetcars

Workers needed public transportation to get to their jobs. The first streetcars were pulled by horses. They only went 3 miles per hour. Next came cable cars, then electric streetcars. Soon, Chicago had the largest streetcar system in the US.

Meatpacking in Chicago

In the early 1900s, Chicago was world-famous for meatpacking. (This poster promoted meat from a Chicago company in France.) This is why the city was called the "hog butcher to the world" in a poem by Carl Sandburg. Most meatpacking was done in the Union Stockyards where workers were treated badly.

The Great Migration

From 1910 to 1930, many African Americans left the southern states and went north. There were few good jobs in the South. Also, black and white people were separated there. Violence between the races was a problem. So, thousands of black people came to Chicago. They could make a fresh start.

Garment industry sweatshop

Before the 1860s, most people made clothes at home. Then, companies in Chicago began to make clothes (garments) to sell in stores. They used immigrants—people who came to Chicago from other countries. The companies made them work long hours for little pay. The shops where they worked were called "sweatshops."

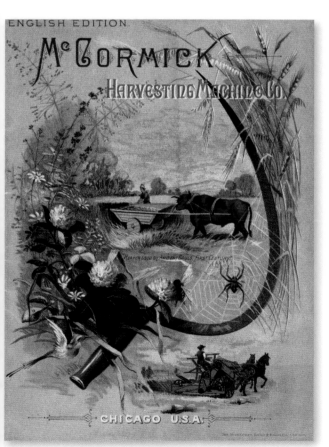

The cover of a McCormick Harvesting Company catalog

Factory production

There are many factories in Chicago. This is a place where goods are made quickly and in large numbers. Some make machine parts; others clothes or food. The Quaker Oats company opened a factory in Chicago in 1901. They are still based here today. They are known for instant oatmeal and breakfast snack bars.

The McCormick reaper

Cyrus McCormick was an inventor. He created a farm machine called a reaper. It could gather as much wheat as three men. Farmers everywhere wanted one. McCormick opened a factory to make reapers in Chicago. He shipped them all over the world.

The Great Chicago Fire

By 1870, Chicago was one of the biggest cities in the United States. More than 300,000 people lived here. It was a center of business and the arts. There were many new streets and buildings. Lots of them were made of wood. The fall of 1871 was very dry. It had not rained in Chicago for many weeks. On October 8, a fire started on the West Side. The wood went up in flames. The strong winds and dry air helped it burn for two days.

Mrs. O'Leary's cow

The fire started in or near Catherine O'Leary's barn. But, how did it start? A boy said Mrs. O'Leary had chased him from the barn and he tipped over a lantern. Others blamed a neighbor, "Peg Leg" Sullivan. One newspaper said a cow started the fire by kicking over a lantern. No one knows for sure.

The fire spreads

Conditions were just right for a fire. The city's wooden buildings were dry because it hadn't rained for weeks. Strong winds meant that the flames moved quickly. The fire spread from the city center to hotels, stores, and many homes. It even spread across the river.

Firemen were tired from putting out another big fire the day before this one.

Putting out the fire

The fire department did not hear about the fire for about 40 minutes. Then, the firefighters were sent to the wrong place. Soon, the fire cut off the city's water supply. Other cities were called to help. But the fire grew too large and firefighters had to give up.

The aftermath

The fire went out by itself after two days. When it was over, 17,500 buildings had burned down. Only five buildings were left in the fire zone. Also, 120 miles of wooden sidewalk had been destroyed. Thousands of people were left homeless. At least 300 people died.

The Palmer House Hotel

Potter Palmer was a wealthy Chicago businessman. He built the Palmer House in 1871. It was a wedding gift for his wife. The hotel was only open for 13 days before it burned down in the fire. Work started on another hotel right away. The new hotel (above) was one of the grandest in Chicago.

Rebuilding the city

THE GREAT CHICAGO FIRE was a huge tragedy. It also gave the city a fresh start. Some of the most talented architects and engineers in the world came here. Building started right away on skyscrapers. Public parks were also created. The city kept building and growing for many years. Daniel Burnham's 1909 Plan of Chicago sought to expand the city. He wanted wider streets and more parks.

Elevated tramway

After many tries, a city train service finally started in 1892. The trains ran on tracks raised above the ground. These were called elevated tracks. They went through alleys behind homes. Soon the train service had a nickname: "the alley L."

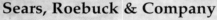

Sears, Roebuck & Company

After the fire, business in Chicago grew quickly. Sears, Roebuck & Company became very successful selling goods by mail. Its first catalog came out in 1888. It sold farm equipment. Soon it also sold toys, food, cars, and even kits to build houses. Sears became one of the biggest companies in the United States.

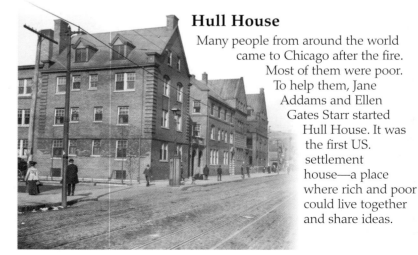

Hull House

Many people from around the world came to Chicago after the fire. Most of them were poor. To help them, Jane Addams and Ellen Gates Starr started Hull House. It was the first US. settlement house—a place where rich and poor could live together and share ideas.

Haymarket riot

Chicago workers wanted to improve their jobs. In May 1886, some went on strike to get a shorter 8-hour workday. They gathered in Haymarket Square, where a fight broke out with police. Eight people were killed. Workers around the world remember that event every year on May Day (May 1).

Robie House

A lot of architects built skyscrapers in Chicago. Others designed "prairie-style" buildings that suited the landscape. One of the most famous is Robie House on the South Side. It was built by Frank Lloyd Wright.

A statue in the West Loop marks the site of the Haymarket riot.

The Chicago World's Fair

CHICAGO HOSTED the World's Fair in 1893. (It was also called the World's Columbian Exposition.) This was a chance for the city to show off how much it had grown since the Great Chicago Fire (see pp24–5). The fair lasted for six months. About 27 million people visited. More than 200 buildings, plus canals and lagoons, were built for the fair. Many new products and inventions were shown here for the first time, too. The people of Chicago were very proud.

For the world, but not for everyone

The World's Fair exhibits were not open to black people. Two leaders of the black community, Frederick Douglass (left) and Ida B. Wells, came to Chicago to protest. Fair leaders decided to allow black people in for one day, called "Negro Day."

The site of the fair in 1893 (now it is Jackson Park)

Chicago Day

Chicago Day was held at the fair on October 9, 1893. It had been 22 years since the Great Chicago Fire. More than 717,000 people came to the fair that day.

Bird's-eye view

Architect Daniel Burnham led building plans for the fair. Most of the buildings were made of bright, white plaster. As a result, the fairgrounds were called the White City. The Palace of Fine Arts building was used after the fair. It was turned into the Field Museum to hold artifacts (see pp42-3).

Heinz pickle pin

The Heinz booth at the fair was in a bad location. So the company gave away small pickle pins to get people to come to see them. It was one of the first times a company had done this. It was a good idea, because crowds came to get the pins.

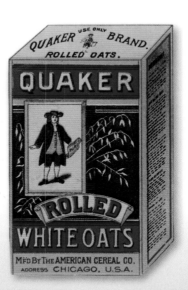

Quaker Oats

Many new foods at the fair could be made quickly or eaten on the go. Quaker Oats was one of them. They could be heated or eaten as oatmeal. The fair was the first place that people ate sausages on buns (hot dogs) and caramel corn with peanuts (Cracker Jack).

Ferris wheel

The biggest attraction at the fair was 264-feet high. It was the first Ferris wheel. Some called it the Chicago Wheel. It had 36 cars, and each car held 60 people. A ride took 20 minutes and cost 50 cents.

Buildings erected all over the country copied the styles at the fair.

Political change

IN MAY 1860, THE REPUBLICAN PARTY met in Chicago. At a meeting hall called the "Wigwam" they nominated Abraham Lincoln for US President. After that, the city changed politically. People moved here from all over the world. They brought different issues to the city. Crime also increased. Gangs were formed and the city became violent. Those in politics became dishonest. The city had to fight for change.

John Dillinger

Dillinger was a bank robber. The police could not stop him. He robbed 10 banks and broke out of jail three times. Finally, in 1934, police trapped Dillinger and shot him dead. He was killed outside Chicago's Biograph Theater.

Prohibition and gangsters

The sale of alcohol became illegal in the United States in 1919. (This law was known as prohibition.) So, many Chicago gangsters made their own alcohol. The most famous was Al Capone. He killed anyone who got in his way. He ordered the shooting of seven men in Lincoln Park. Their murder was called the St. Valentine's Day Massacre.

Chicago Race Riot, 1919

Conflicts between black people and white people became very bad during the summer of 1919. For eight days, the two groups attacked each other. The homes of some black families were burned down. Many of them packed up and moved out of Chicago.

Mayoral firsts

In 1979, Chicago elected its first woman mayor. Her name was Jane Byrne (right). Jane had many problems during her term. In 1983, she was replaced by Harold Washington. He was the city's first African American mayor.

Protesters waved flags of the Viet Cong, America's enemy in the Vietnam War.

MLK in Chicago

Martin Luther King, Jr., came to Chicago in 1966 to help black people. They wanted better schools and places to live. MLK moved into a run-down building to show how bad things were. He also led marches and gave speeches.

The whole world is watching

In 1968, the Democratic Party held its convention in Chicago. They came to nominate a candidate for President. Many people protested in the streets. They were angry about the Vietnam War. The protesters fought with police, who sprayed tear gas. TV cameras filmed the fight. Protestors shouted "the whole world is watching."

The Jazz Age

The Original Dixieland Jazz Band

This New Orleans-style jazz band formed in Chicago in 1916. They played at a club called Schiller's Café. They were a fast hit. Their song "Livery Stable Blues" was the first jazz record single ever released.

By the 1920s, jazz music was becoming popular all across America. Chicago had one of the most exciting music scenes in the country. Many African Americans had come to Chicago from the south during the Great Migration (see p22). They brought music traditions with them. The city was the place where many famous musicians lived, recorded music and played in jazz clubs. Musicians such as Louis Armstrong and Jelly Roll Morton made names for themselves here, then moved on to New York City and bigger fame.

King Oliver's Creole Jazz Band

Joe "King" Oliver was a jazz cornet player and bandleader. His band introduced the Dixieland style of jazz music to Chicago. Louis Armstrong played with him (see opposite page).

Louis Armstrong, slide trumpet player

Baby Dodds, drummer

King Oliver, cornet player

Bill Johnson, banjo player

Johnny Dodds, clarinetist

Honore Dutrey, trombone player

Lil Hardin, pianist

Kazoo

The kazoo is a small wind instrument. When you hum into it, the kazoo makes a buzzy noise. It used to be an important instrument in jazz music. It was used for many solos.

Jelly Roll Morton

Morton was a jazz pianist and a bandleader. (His real name was Ferdinand Joseph LaMothe.) His song "Wolverine Blues" was a big hit in Chicago. He released his first set of recordings when he lived here. Some were with his band, Jelly Roll Morton & His Red Hot Peppers.

Count Basie and His Orchestra

William "Count" Basie was a jazz songwriter. He also played the piano and led a big band for almost 50 years. His band stayed in Chicago from 1936 to 1937. They played many shows at the Grand Terrace Ballroom.

Louis Armstrong's first cornet

Louis Armstrong

This jazz singer and trumpet player was born in New Orleans. He joined King Oliver in Chicago. Louis Armstrong became very famous on his own. He recorded songs here with two groups, the Hot Five and the Hot Seven. He is considered to be one of the best trumpet players of all time.

One of Louis Armstrong's early jazz records

Multicultural Chicago

PEOPLE FROM ALL OVER THE WORLD live in Chicago. More than 130 languages are spoken here. Little Italy, Chinatown, and Greektown are neighborhoods that represent ethnic groups. They have their own styles of food and music. There are many festivals in Chicago that celebrate different cultures. The city's museums also have exhibitions that show how different people are. It is said that you can "see the world" just by coming to Chicago.

Puerto Rican Passage

A mile-long section of Division Street is called Paseo Boricua, or the Puerto Rican Passage. It is marked on both ends by 59-feet-tall Puerto Rican flag sculptures. Many people from Chicago's Puerto Rican community live in this part of the Humboldt Park neighborhood.

The murals of Pilsen

Pilsen is a South Side neighborhood. Many Mexican people live there. Pilsen is known for its murals. A mural is a large wall painting that tells a story. Murals are a popular form of art in Mexico. They make Pilsen seem like an outdoor museum.

Bronzeville

Bronzeville is a famous neighborhood in Chicago. It grew quickly when many African Americans settled there during the Great Migration. It soon became the center of Chicago's black culture. Many famous African Americans lived and worked there. The musician Louis Armstrong and poet Gwendolyn Brooks are two of them.

Devon Avenue

Devon Avenue is a long road on the North Side. Many different cultures live along this one road. From the west, it begins as an Orthodox Jewish neighborhood. Moving east, it becomes Russian. After that, it turns into an Indian and Pakistani area.

Pilsen's murals cover many subjects, including Mexican heroes and local people.

Chinatown Gate is a famous landmark in Chicago's Chinatown.

Chinatown

Chinatown is on the South Side. It is filled with Chinese restaurants and shops. There is a park with a bamboo garden, as well as outdoor art. A Chinese New Year parade takes place every February. In summer, there is a dragon boat race.

Skyscrapers

THE GREAT CHICAGO FIRE OF 1871 wiped out most of the city (see pp24–5). There were very few buildings left so architects had a fresh start. They used new materials and designs. Some created buildings that were taller than the world had ever seen. Since then, Chicago has kept building bigger. Today, it is home to many of the tallest skyscrapers in the United States and the world.

World's first skyscraper

The Home Insurance Building was built in 1885. It was just 10 stories tall. Still, it is considered to be the world's first skyscraper because it was the first tall building made with a light steel frame. Before this, tall buildings were made with heavy stone.

The Reliance Building

The Reliance Building was built between 1890 and 1895. It was the first building to be made using mostly steel and glass. Now, many buildings are made with these materials. The 14-story building is famous for its "Chicago windows." These are large glass panels that cover the outside. Today, this building is known as the Hotel Burnham.

Willis Tower (1,451 feet)

AT&T Corporate Center (1,007 feet)

CNA Plaza (601 feet)

Chase Tower (850 feet)

Willis Tower

Willis Tower is the tallest building in the US. It is also the fifth-tallest building in the world. It was built in 1973. Willis Tower was called the Sears Tower until 2009. It has 108 floors and is 1,451 feet tall (although one of its antennae reaches 1,730 feet). Many Chicago radio and television stations have transmitters at the top.

Willis Tower

Trump International Hotel and Tower

The Trump Tower is the newest skyscraper in Chicago. It was built in 2009 and stands at 1,389 feet. It is the second-tallest building in the US, after the Willis Tower. It is a hotel, but people also live there. In fact, some people live above the 89th floor. Those are the highest "homes" in the world.

Smurfitt Stone Building (582 feet)

Two Prudential Plaza (995 feet)

AON Center (1,136 feet)

John Hancock Center (1,127 feet)

Water Tower Place (859 feet)

Transportation

The CTA

The Chicago Transit Authority (CTA) runs the trains and buses in Chicago and some suburbs. Passengers pay the fare to ride using cards like this one.

CHICAGO'S LOCATION in the middle of the country makes it a busy transportation hub. Lots of people and goods come through here on their way to other places. They use planes, trains, buses, and cars. Transportation within the city is important, too. Almost 10 million people live in and around Chicago. There is a good public transport network to help them all get around.

Cycling

Chicago is a bicycle-friendly city. There are lots of bike lanes on the roads. On the lakefront there is a pretty bicycle path. There is also a cycle center in Millennium Park. Bikers can come here to park, shower, make repairs, and rent bicycles.

Lake Shore Drive

This highway runs alongside Lake Michigan. It goes from the North Side to the South Side of the city. Lake Shore Drive was first intended for walking and carriage rides by rich Chicagoans. Then, cars became popular, allowing everyone to use the Drive.

Freight

Much of the freight that moves across the country travels through Chicago. It runs along miles of railroad tracks. These tracks go in and around the city. Train tunnels go underground. The city also has bridges for trains to get across the water.

The "L"

The CTA runs L trains (L is short for "elevated"). The red and blue lines run 24 hours a day. There are eight train lines, each named for a color. Some of the tracks are high above the ground. Others are below ground, in tunnels.

Airports

There are two major airports in the Chicago area. O'Hare is on the North Side. It's one of the busiest airports in the world. More than 2,400 flights come through here each day. Midway Airport is a smaller airport on the South Side.

Banking boom

By the mid-1800s, Chicago was known for making goods. The city could also move those goods anywhere in the country. The Chicago Board of Trade was opened in 1848 to buy and sell farm products. Another trading floor, the Chicago Mercantile Exchange, opened in 1898. Banks were also needed to deal with the money being made. The First National Bank of Chicago opened in 1868. By 1900, Chicago was an important banking center like New York City and London, UK.

Bank vault

By the 1920s, Chicago was one of the greatest banking centers in the world. Its banks dealt with money for many businesses. There were also banks for people to use. Steel "vaults" protected their money. They also had secret lock boxes for people's personal items.

Chicago Board of Trade

This is the oldest place to trade goods in the United States. Traders here buy and sell products, such as silver, that will be delivered later ("futures"). They also pay for the right to buy and sell things ("options"). Some traders stand in a "pit" where they watch prices and shout deals.

First National Bank of Chicago

In 1862, a group of people wanted to start a bank. They came up with $250,000 and opened First National Bank of Chicago. It soon became the city's largest bank. It was also the first bank in the country to offer banking to women.

Chicago Mercantile Exchange

"The Merc" is also a place where goods are traded. Here, farm products (like cows and pigs) are bought and sold. Some use the pit and others do electronic trading on computers. Workers here wear different color jackets to show what job they do.

Federal Reserve Bank of Chicago

The US "central bank" is split up into 12 smaller banks. These banks are called "reserves." One of the reserves is here in Chicago. The Chicago reserve deals with the money needs of five states. It even has a Money Museum. Here, visitors can take their picture next to $1 million in cash.

Great museums

CHICAGO IS HOME TO some of the biggest museums in the country. Many have treasures you can't find anywhere else in the world. For example, there is a real spacecraft used by astronauts. The world's most complete dinosaur skeleton is also here. There is even a German submarine from World War II. The Field Museum, Adler Planetarium, and Shedd Aquarium make up the Museum Campus. The campus is an area on the lakefront.

Adler Planetarium
This is the oldest operating planetarium in the world. You can learn all about astronomy here. There are three theaters for viewing the stars and the sky, plus a museum. The *Gemini 12* spacecraft used by astronauts is on display here.

Shedd Aquarium
At the Shedd, you can see sea life as small as snails and as big as whales. Other creatures include penguins and dolphins. To hold them all, the aquarium uses more than 5 million gallons of water.

Museum of Science and Industry

The MSI's giant, walk-through heart is 13 feet tall. You can program it with your pulse so that it beats in sync with your own heart.

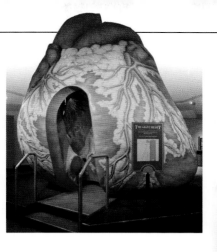

Art Institute of Chicago

There are more than 260,000 paintings at the Art Institute. They come from Asia, Europe, and America. Many are by famous artists. They include Claude Monet, Vincent Van Gogh, and Edward Hopper. A new Modern Wing has an area just for kids to learn about art.

Field Museum

The Field looks at the natural world. The museum has 21 million items. Some of these include jewels, ancient tools, and animal exhibits. Its most famous resident is Sue, the most complete T.rex skeleton found so far.

Chicago History Museum

This is one of the city's oldest museums. It was built in 1856. It burned down in the Great Chicago Fire (see pp24–5), but was rebuilt. Today, you can see the *Pioneer* train (see pp18–19) and the first "L" car here.

University of Chicago

THE UNIVERSITY OF CHICAGO is in Hyde Park on the South Side of Chicago. The millionaire John D. Rockefeller donated money to build the school. It opened in 1892, at a time when the city was growing bigger and bigger. Today, it is ranked as one of the best universities in the United States. Many Nobel Prize winners have come from here. The school is also famous for the research it does in science and other areas.

Henry Moore sculpture

This sculpture is called *Nuclear Energy*. It marks the site where scientists made the first controlled, self-sustaining nuclear chain reaction. It took place in 1945 and led to the creation of the atomic bomb. Many people say Henry Moore's sculpture looks like a human skull or a mushroom cloud.

Regenstein Library

The university's main library has almost 4.5 million books. There are big collections of maps and children's books. The books are stored away from the reading area. A cool temperature helps them last longer.

Oriental Institute Museum

Five galleries make up this archaeology museum. There are artifacts here from Egypt, Israel, Turkey, and other Middle East countries. One of the most famous artifacts is a 17-foot statue of King Tut that is thought to be 3,000 years old.

SEPH REGENSTEIN LIBRARY

Cobb Gate gargoyles

Stone carvings called "gargoyles" are found on Cobb Gate, one of the university's main entrances. They sit at different heights on the gate. They represent students studying for four years in college.

Smart Museum of Art

This small, free museum on the University of Chicago campus was founded in 1974. Its collection has more than 10,000 works of art. These include pieces by Frank Lloyd Wright, Edgar Degas, and Pablo Picasso.

Angel with harp at Bond Chapel

Bond Chapel

The school chapel opened in 1926. Its stained glass windows were added in 1949. On the outside, there are many stone carvings. Some of them include Adam and Eve, angels, lions, and dragons. Some say they represent a struggle between good and bad.

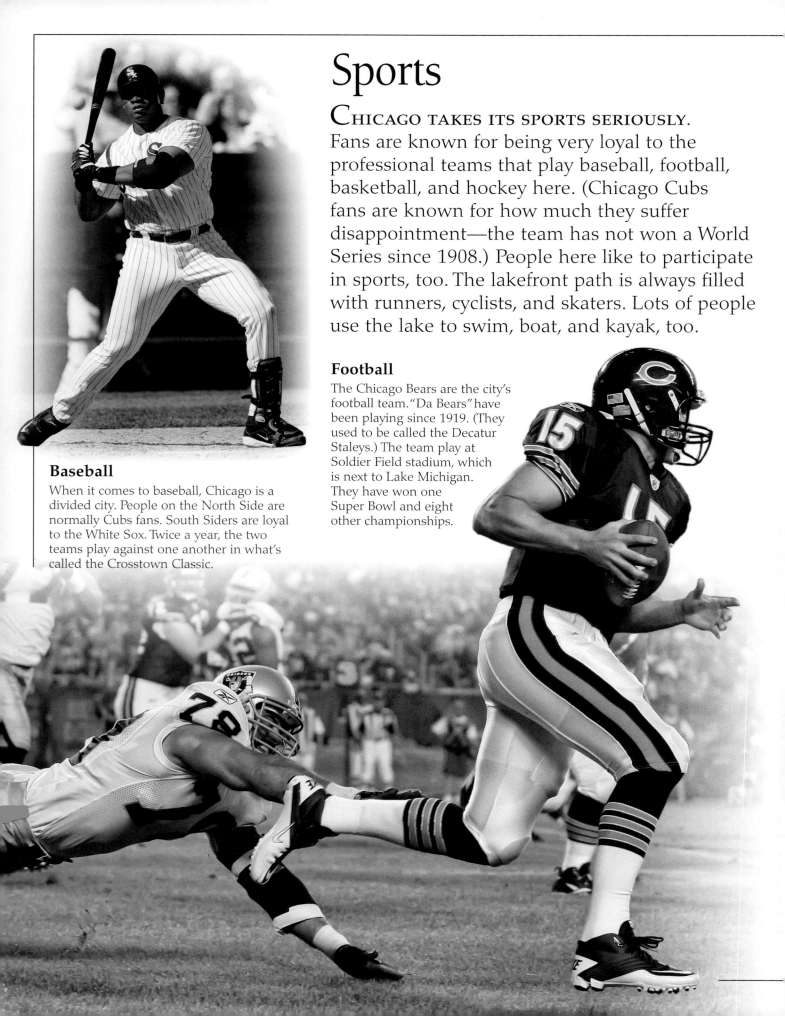

Sports

CHICAGO TAKES ITS SPORTS SERIOUSLY. Fans are known for being very loyal to the professional teams that play baseball, football, basketball, and hockey here. (Chicago Cubs fans are known for how much they suffer disappointment—the team has not won a World Series since 1908.) People here like to participate in sports, too. The lakefront path is always filled with runners, cyclists, and skaters. Lots of people use the lake to swim, boat, and kayak, too.

Baseball

When it comes to baseball, Chicago is a divided city. People on the North Side are normally Cubs fans. South Siders are loyal to the White Sox. Twice a year, the two teams play against one another in what's called the Crosstown Classic.

Football

The Chicago Bears are the city's football team. "Da Bears" have been playing since 1919. (They used to be called the Decatur Staleys.) The team play at Soldier Field stadium, which is next to Lake Michigan. They have won one Super Bowl and eight other championships.

Chicago Blackhawks

The Blackhawks are the city's National Hockey League (NHL) team. They are one of the original six teams that began playing in this league in 1942. The "Hawks" have won the Stanley Cup four times, including in 2010.

Chicago Bulls

The Chicago Bulls were founded in 1966 and play at the United Center. During the 1990s, the basketball team was very successful. The players included Michael Jordan (nicknamed "His Airness" for his high jumps) and Scottie Pippen. They won six championships.

Race to Mackinac

This yearly sailboat race starts where the Chicago River meets Lake Michigan and ends at Mackinac Island in Michigan. It is about 333 miles long, making it one of the longest freshwater sailboat races in the world.

Chicago Marathon

The 26.2-mile Chicago marathon is held every October. It was first held in 1905. Then, there were only 20 runners. Now, about 45,000 people run it each year. The world record for fastest time has been broken at this race more than once.

Entertainment

YOU CAN SEE WORLD-CLASS theater, music, comedy, and dance in Chicago. Performers are known for putting on brilliant shows and doing things that you can't see anywhere else. Many famous entertainers got their start in Chicago. This is a great place to see small, locally produced shows. The city is also home to large, older theaters that have fancy set designs and amazing costumes.

Steppenwolf Theatre Company

Steppenwolf was founded in 1974 by three Chicago actors. The company is famous for producing award-winning plays. These include *August! Osage County* (2007) and *The Grapes of Wrath* (1988). Both of these shows won the national Tony Award for Best Play.

Dancers make unusual shapes with their bodies.

The Second City

Chicago is known as the training ground for the best comics in the world, because of The Second City. It is an improv group, which means the performers "improvise," or make things up as they go along. John Candy, Tina Fey, and Steve Carrell are some of the famous comics who started here.

River North Dance Chicago

River North is a modern jazz dance company. It was set up in 1989 by four dancers. It is now one of Chicago's most well-known dance groups. The company performs all over the US. It also puts on shows in other countries. Modern jazz is a fast style of dance. It is based on ballet and jazz music.

Puppet Bike

This is a good example of the quirky performances you can see in Chicago. Puppet Bike is a small stage attached to a bicycle. Performers ride around town and stage outdoor puppet shows for anyone who will stop to watch.

Chicago Theatre

The Chicago Theatre was built in 1921. It started as a very fancy movie house and was one of the first to use air conditioning. The inside is decorated with large chandeliers and murals. There are nearly 4,000 seats.

The media

CHICAGO IS THE THIRD-LARGEST media market in the United States. (Only New York City and Los Angeles are bigger.) That means that the television stations, radio stations, newspapers, magazines, and local websites here serve the third-largest number of people. The Tribune Company, which owns the Chicago Tribune, is based here. It runs some of the biggest newspapers in the world. Important media figures, such as Oprah Winfrey and Roger Ebert, made names for themselves in Chicago.

Television studios

Some local television stations have news studios at street level. People walking downtown can stop and watch live news broadcasts through the window. Both WLS (channel 7) and WBBM (channel 2) have this type of studio.

Oprah Winfrey

For 25 years, Oprah Winfrey hosted and produced a talk show from Chicago. The last episode was in 2011. Her studio, called Harpo Studios, is in the West Loop. "Harpo" is "Oprah" spelled backward.

Roger Ebert

Roger Ebert is one of the most famous movie critics in the country. He writes for the *Chicago Sun-Times* newspaper. His reviews also appear in hundreds of other newspapers. Ebert has been on many television shows that review movies.

Tribune Tower

This building is the home of the *Chicago Tribune* newspaper. It is the most successful newspaper in the Midwest. The lower parts of the building include rocks and bricks from other famous places. These places include the Great Wall of China and Abraham Lincoln's tomb. They were brought back by "Trib" reporters.

Movie locations

Chicago is a popular place to film movies. Some scenes from the Batman movie *The Dark Knight* (above) were filmed downtown. Other famous movies that were filmed here include *Transformers 3*, *The Blues Brothers*, and *Home Alone*.

Famous food

CHICAGO IS A GOOD CITY to be hungry in. The foods it is most known for are hot dogs and deep-dish pizza, but there are many other delicious things to eat here, too. There are world-class steak houses and fancy restaurants run by famous chefs. There are also many farmers' markets that sell fresh fruits and vegetables. You can also find foods from all over the world made by people who have come here from other countries.

Maxwell Street

A Maxwell Street Polish is classic Chicago street food. This grilled sausage sandwich is usually topped with onions, mustard, and sometimes peppers. It is thought to have been first served at Maxwell Street Market, a famous flea market on the South Side.

Farmers' markets

During the summer, there are many outdoor farmers' markets in Chicago. Some are downtown near office buildings and others are in neighborhoods. One of the best known is Green City Market. This market is in Lincoln Park. Many chefs shop for organic fruits and vegetables here.

Italian beef

Italian beef sandwiches are a popular Chicago food. They're made with roast beef and served "wet" (dipped in the meat's juices) or "dry" (not dipped). You can also order them "hot" (with giardiniera, a spicy, pickled mix of vegetables) and "sweet" (topped with sweet peppers).

Tomato

Mustard

Sport peppers

Relish

Chopped onions

Pickle spear

Hot dogs

Chicago hot dogs are eaten on poppy seed buns. They are "dragged through the garden." This means that they are topped with lots of vegetables. The toppings became popular during the Great Depression. They made for a cheap, filling meal.

Deep-dish pizza

Chicago-style deep-dish pizza was invented in 1943 at Pizzeria Uno. It is usually a few inches deep and filled with cheese and ingredients such as sausage and vegetables. Sauce is put on top. You need a knife and fork to eat this pizza.

Orange sherbet

Pistachio

Palmer House

Strawberry

Chocolate

Original Rainbow Cone

The Original Rainbow Cone is a South Side ice-cream shop. It opened in 1926. Its famous, jumbo-sized ice-cream cone has five flavors. They are chocolate, strawberry, Palmer House (vanilla with cherries and walnuts), pistachio, and orange sherbet.

THE ORIGINAL RAINBOW CONE

EST. 1926

Events and attractions

CHICAGO IS A CITY WHERE YOU will never be bored. No matter what your interests, it's easy to find something to do here. There are fairs, festivals, concerts, and shows year-round. There are also plenty of museums, parks, gardens, and beaches to visit. The city is especially busy during the summer months when there are lots of outdoor events. This is when the long, cold winter is over and people enjoy spending as much time outside as they can.

Lollapalooza

This is an annual three-day music festival that happens in Grant Park every summer. Indie, punk rock, and pop music acts from around the world play here. "Kidzapalooza" is a festival within the festival with music and activities just for kids.

Chicago Botanic Garden

The beautiful Chicago Botanic Garden is in the northern suburb of Glencoe. There are 24 gardens here, including a traditional English garden. There is also a railroad garden where model trains travel through buildings made of plants and branches.

Oak Street Beach

This beach is steps from the skyscrapers along Michigan Avenue. There are volleyball courts, restaurants, and bicycle and running paths. Swimmers and scuba divers also come here. It is one of the city's most popular beaches.

Summer street festivals

Summer in Chicago means street festivals. There are festivals just about every weekend. These outdoor parties celebrate the culture of each neighborhood. There is usually a variety of food and music. One of the most popular is Taste of Chicago. This event lasts for 10 days. It is the world's largest food festival.

Chicago Air and Water Show

More than 2 million people come to the area around North Avenue Beach every August to see this free show. It features boats and planes doing tricks. The US Navy's Blue Angels and the US Air Force Thunderbirds take turns as the final act each year.

Green city

CHICAGO IS A VERY "GREEN" CITY. It has 12,000 acres of public parks and waterfront space. People here take care to protect the environment. There are lots of paths to encourage bike riding instead of driving. The city has a recycling program and helps to build homes that use low amounts of energy. Chicago has also planted over 2 million square feet of rooftop gardens. That's more than all the other cities in the United States combined!

Green roofs

Many buildings in Chicago have plants on the rooftops. The plants provide shade in hot weather and keep the warm air inside during winter. This means the buildings use less energy for heating and cooling. City Hall, which is a government building, has a 20,000-square-foot green roof (above).

Bike riding

Riding a bike is a green way of getting around. That's because bikes don't give out exhaust fumes. Chicago is one of the best cities in the country for riding. Former Mayors Richard J. and Richard M. Daley both supported cycling. They built lots of bike paths. Now, many people ride to work. On the last Friday of every month, thousands of cyclists ride through the city for fun.

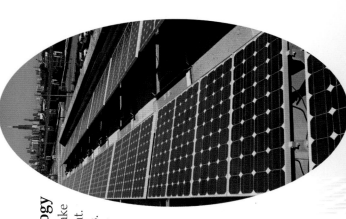

Center for Green Technology

Here, Chicagoans can learn how to make their homes better for the environment. The center offers classes and tours. It is also a recycling center. The building has a green roof and uses solar panels to get heat from the sun.

City in bloom

Many of Chicago's public spaces are covered in flowers. There are several free, public gardens that have indoor and outdoor spaces. You can also see flowers along big streets and highways. In Chicago, flowers are planted wherever possible.

Famous Chicagoans

ACTORS AND ARTISTS

John and Joan Cusack

These actors are brother and sister. They were born and raised in the suburb of Evanston. They both went to the Piven Theatre Workshop, run by the parents of actor Jeremy Piven.

Jennifer Hudson

The American Idol contestant won an Oscar for her role in the movie *Dreamgirls*. She was born and raised in Chicago, and still lives here.

Bernie Mac

The comedian famous for being one of "The Original Kings of Comedy" was born in Chicago. He lived here until his death in 2008.

Bill Murray

This well-known actor and comedian was born in the suburb of Wilmette. He started his career as part of the Second City comedy troupe (see p48).

Johnny Weissmuller

Weissmuller was famous for playing Tarzan in movies that were made during the 1930s and 1940s. Before that, he was a gold-medal winning Olympic swimmer.

Jennifer Hudson

MUSICIANS

Louis Armstrong

Armstrong was both a trumpet player and singer. He was part of Chicago's famous Jazz Age during the 1920s.

Nat "King" Cole

This big-band singer was one of the first black Americans to host a television variety show. He grew up in the Bronzeville neighborhood.

Common

This hip-hop artist and actor is from the South Side of Chicago.

Billy Corgan

The lead singer of Smashing Pumpkins lives in the Lake View neighborhood.

Buddy Guy

This blues guitarist and singer has a club, Buddy Guy's Legends, in the South Loop.

Jeff Tweedy

The lead singer of the rock band Wilco lives in Chicago. His son, Spencer, is in the teen band The Blisters.

Jeff Tweedy

AUTHORS AND JOURNALISTS

Gwendolyn Brooks

This African American poet won a lot of awards for her work, including the Pulitzer Prize. Her first book of poems was called *A Street in Bronzeville*. She lived in Chicago for most of her life.

Roger Ebert

The famous film critic has worked for the *Chicago Sun-Times* newspaper since 1967 (see p50).

Ernest Hemingway

Hemingway is one of America's most famous writers. He wrote *The Sun Also Rises* and *The Old Man and the Sea*. He was born and raised in Oak Park, a suburb of Chicago.

Shel Silverstein

The poet who wrote the children's books *The Giving Tree* and *The Missing Piece* was born and raised in Chicago.

Studs Terkel

This author and historian is best known for his stories about everyday Chicagoans. He won the Pulitzer Prize in 1985 and died in 2008.

Oprah Winfrey

The legendary talk-show host produced *The Oprah Winfrey Show* in Chicago for 25 years. Her company, Harpo Studios, is in the West Loop neighborhood (see p50).

POLITICAL AND RELIGIOUS LEADERS

SPORTS FIGURES

Bobby Hull

Richard J. and Richard M. Daley

This father-son pair served the longest terms as Chicago mayors. Richard J. served for 21 years until he died in 1976. Richard M. served for 22 years, from 1989 until he retired in 2011.

Jesse Jackson

The civil rights activist and minister runs the Rainbow/PUSH organization from Chicago.

Hillary Clinton

Hillary Clinton was First Lady of the United States from 1993 until 2001. She was born in Chicago and raised in the suburb of Park Ridge. Then she was a United States Senator for New York. In 2009, she became Secretary of State.

Barack and Michelle Obama

The 44th President and First Lady of the United States are from Chicago. Michelle Obama was born here, but the President was born in Hawaii. They still have a house in the Kenwood neighborhood.

Harry Caray

Caray was the announcer for the Chicago Cubs baseball team. He was famous for singing "Take Me Out to the Ballgame" during the seventh inning stretch at Wrigley Field. He died in 1998.

Mike Ditka

"Iron Mike" coached the Chicago Bears for 11 years. He led the football team to a Super Bowl championship in 1986.

Bobby Hull

The man nicknamed "the Golden Jet" played for the Chicago Blackhawks from 1957 until 1972. He was left wing for the ice hockey team. He helped the Hawks to win the Stanley Cup in 1961.

Michael Jordan

Jordan is considered by many to be the greatest basketball player of all time. He won six NBA championships playing with the Chicago Bulls.

Walter Peyton

"Sweetness" played for the Chicago Bears for his whole career, from 1975 until 1987. His style and speed helped make him a great player.

US President Barack Obama

First Lady Michelle Obama

Questions and answers

Q Why is there a large aluminum owl atop the Harold Washington Library in downtown Chicago?

A The owl is the Greek symbol for knowledge.

Owl sculpture

Q Crown Fountain is an art and video sculpture in Millennium Park. It spouts water from the images of people's mouths into a pool. Whose faces are on the sculpture?

A The faces are of 75 people chosen from all over Chicago.

Crown Fountain

Q Buckingham Fountain is one of the largest fountains in the world and sits in Chicago's "front yard" in Grant Park. There are four seahorses around the fountain. Why are they there?

A The four seahorses represent the four states that border Lake Michigan: Illinois, Indiana, Michigan, and Wisconsin.

Buckingham Fountain

Q The State of Illinois is nicknamed the "Land of Lincoln." Abraham Lincoln spent a lot of time in Chicago and other parts of the state, but he was not born here. What state was he born in?

A Kentucky.

Abraham Lincoln

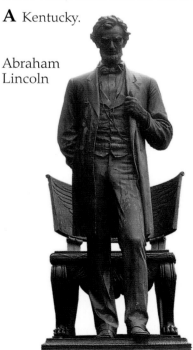

The clock at Marshall Field's

Q The famous Marshall Field's department store is still at the corner of State and Washington streets, but the store it is attached to is no longer Marshall Field's. What is it now called?

A Macy's.

Dearborn Station

Q Dearborn Station was one of six railroad stations in Chicago in the late 1800s. Today, trains no longer travel there. What is the station used for now?

A It houses stores and offices.

Questions and answers

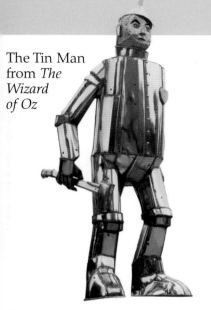

The Tin Man from *The Wizard of Oz*

Q Oz Park in the Lincoln Park neighborhood has sculptures of many of the characters from the movie *The Wizard of Oz*. Do you know why they are here?

A The author of *The Wizard of Oz*, L. Frank Baum, lived near the site where the park is today.

Q There are two bronze lions that stand guard outside of the Art Institute. How are they different?

A They are standing in different positions. According to the museum, the north lion "is on the prowl" and the south one "stands in an attitude of defiance."

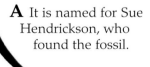

Lion statue, Art Institute

Wrigley Field stadium entrance

Q Wrigley Field is where the Chicago Cubs play. It was the last Major League Baseball stadium to do something very important. What was it?

A The stadium did not have lights until 1988. Before then, no night games could be played here.

Sue, the T. rex skeleton

Q Why is the huge Tyrannosaurus Rex fossil at the Field Museum called Sue?

A It is named for Sue Hendrickson, who found the fossil.

Q The John Hancock Center is the sixth-tallest building in the United States. How many buildings are taller than the Hancock in Chicago?

A Three:
1. Willis Tower
2. Trump International Hotel and Tower
3. The Aon Center

John Hancock Center

Fascinating facts

■ Chicago is the third-largest city in the United States, after New York City and Los Angeles. For many years it was the second-largest city, which is why one of its nicknames is "The Second City."

■ On a clear day, you can see four states from Skydeck Chicago at the top of the Willis Tower: Illinois, Indiana, Michigan, and Wisconsin.

■ The elevators at the Willis Tower travel at a speed of 1,600 feet per minute.

■ After the city of Warsaw, more Polish people live in Chicago than any other city in the world.

■ The world's largest public library is the Harold Washington Branch of the Chicago Public Library at 400 South State Street (below). It contains more than two million books.

■ Chicago loves a parade: more than 200 take place here every year.

■ Western Avenue is one of the longest streets in the world. It measures 24.5 miles from start to finish.

■ The Chicago River is dyed green every year for St. Patrick's Day.

■ Chicago hot dogs have many toppings, but they never, ever include ketchup.

■ Route 66 begins in Chicago and ends in Santa Monica, California.

■ The Nabisco plant in Chicago is the largest bakery in the world. Oreos, Nutter Butters, Chips Ahoy!, and Ritz crackers are made here.

CITY OF NICKNAMES

Chicago has many nicknames—here are just some of them:

◆ The Windy City

◆ The Second City

◆ Hog Butcher to the World

◆ The City That Works

◆ City of Big Shoulders

■ There are many ideas about how Chicago got its name. It was first called "chickagou" by local Indian tribes. Some people believe that they named it for a wild onion that grew here. Others think that it was named for a skunk. The Indian word for skunk was "shegahg." In general, the words all have a meaning that translates to "bad smell."

■ The last time the Chicago Cubs won a World Series was in 1908.

GREAT INVENTIONS

These five objects were all first made in Chicago:

1 Roller skates (1884)

2 The skyscraper (1885)

3 Cracker Jacks (1893)

4 The zipper (1896)

5 The remote control (1950)

■ The world's first Ferris wheel was built in Chicago for the World's Fair in 1893. A Ferris wheel modeled after that one is now at Navy Pier.

■ The game of 16-inch softball, which is played without gloves, was invented in Chicago.

■ The Chicago Bears are named for the first animal at Lincoln Park Zoo, a bear cub that was purchased for $10 in 1874.

Glossary

ARCHITECT A person who designs buildings and houses.

ASTRONOMY The study of the universe and the stars, planets, and galaxies inside of it.

CABLE CAR A car that is pulled along tracks by a cable above it.

CANAL A body of water created by people.

CIVIL RIGHTS Freedoms that all people should have.

COMMODITY A valuable or useful object.

CRITIC A person who judges things, such as movies, plays, and music and decides how good and bad they are.

DIESEL A type of gasoline.

DRAWBRIDGE A bridge that can be raised or lowered to let things go under it.

DUNE A hill that is usually made of sand.

ENGINEER A person who uses science and math to solve problems and make plans.

FREIGHT Goods that are carried by a vehicle, such as a train, or vessel, such as a boat.

FUTURES Products that will be delivered later. Futures are bought and sold at a commodities (or stock) exchange.

GARGOYLE A stone statue of a scary creature on the side of a building. Most gargoyles have spouts, or holes, at their mouths to let rainwater spray out.

GLACIER A very large sheet of ice that moves very slowly over land.

HUB The center of activity.

IMPROV A type of theater where actors make the drama up as they go along.

LAGOON A body of water that is separated from a larger body of water by sand.

MAMMOTH A large, hairy animal related to the elephant. Mammoths lived during the Ice Age. They are now extinct.

MARATHON A 26.2 mile running race.

MASTODON A very large animal that looks like an elephant. Mastodons lived during the Ice Age. They are now extinct.

MIGRATION The movement of people from one country or faraway place to another.

MISSIONARY A person who travels to another country to do religious or charitable work.

MURAL A very large painting that is painted directly on a wall or ceiling.

OPTIONS The rights to buy or sell commodities. Options are traded at a stock exchange.

PLANETARIUM A building that houses a projector that shows the positions of the stars and planets on a domed ceiling.

PORTAGE A land route between two bodies of water, across which boats and equipment can be carried. The word also means the carrying of boats and equipment.

PROHIBITION A law that forbids the sale or drinking of alcohol. Prohibition was a law in the United States from 1920 to 1933.

PROTEST To strongly disagree with something. When groups stage protests they can be peaceful, carrying signs and chanting. However, sometimes protests can be violent, ending in fights and people getting hurt.

REAPER A machine that harvests, or collects, wheat.

RIOT A group act of violence, or fighting.

RIVAL A competitor that wants the same goal.

SETTLEMENT HOUSE A center, often in a poor area, that provides help and services to the community.

SETTLER A person who is one of the first to move to an area.

STANLEY CUP A trophy that is awarded to the winner of the National Hockey League playoffs each year. It is a large bowl made of silver. It is a tradition that the team that wins the Stanley Cup drinks champagne from it.

SWEATSHOP A factory or business where workers have to work long hours in unsafe conditions.

SWING BRIDGE A bridge that moves from side to side to allow boats to pass.

TRANSMITTER An electric device that receives and sends out radio or television signals. There are transmitters at the top of skyscrapers to help signals travel many miles. These signals provide the different channels on your radio and television sets.

VAULT A large room made of steel where people keep money and valuable items.

Index

AB

Addams, Jane, 26
Adler Planetarium, 8, 42
African Americans, 22, 32, 35
airports, 39
Armstrong, Louis, 7, 32, 33, 35, 58
Art Institute of Chicago, 8, 43
banks, 40–41
baseball, 9, 46
Basie, William "Count," 33
basketball, 46, 47
beaches, 54
bison, 10
Black Hawk, Chief, 14, 15, 17
Bond Chapel, 45
bridges, 20, 39
Bronzeville, 35
Brookfield Zoo, 8
Brooks, Gwendolyn, 35, 58
Burnham, Daniel, 26, 28
Byrne, Jane, 31

CD

Calumet Harbor, 21
canals, 12, 13, 20, 21, 28
Capone, Al, 30
Caray, Harry, 59
Center for Green Technology, 56
Chicago, Lake, 11
Chicago Air and Water Show, 55
Chicago Bears, 9, 46, 62
Chicago Blackhawks, 9, 47
Chicago Board of Trade, 40
Chicago Botanic Garden, 54
Chicago Bulls, 9, 47
Chicago Cubs, 9, 46, 62
Chicago Day, 28
Chicago History Museum, 18, 43
Chicago Marathon, 9, 47
Chicago Mercantile Exchange, 40, 41

Chicago Portage, 12
Chicago River, 6, 8, 13, 16, 17, 20, 21, 62
Chicago Theatre, 49
Chicago Transit Authority (CTA), 38, 39
Chicago Tribune, 50, 51
"Chicagoland," 8
Chinatown, 34, 35
City Hall, 8, 56
Clinton, Hillary, 59
Cole, Nat "King," 58
Common, 58
Corgan, Billy, 58
crime, 30
Cusack, John and Joan, 58
cycling, 38, 46, 56
Daley, Richard J. and Richard M., 56, 59
dance, 48–49
Democratic Party, 31
Devon Avenue, 35
Dillinger, John, 30
Ditka, Mike, 59
Douglass, Frederick, 28
Du Sable, Jean Baptiste Point, 17

EFG

Ebert, Roger, 50, 58
elevated tramway, 26, 39
entertainment, 48–49
events, 54–55
explorers, 16–17
factories, 22–23
farmers' markets, 52
Federal Reserve Bank of Chicago, 41
Ferris wheel, 9, 29, 62
festivals, 34, 54–55
Field Museum of Natural History, 8, 28, 42, 43
First National Bank of Chicago, 40, 41
flag, 6
flowers, 56–57
food, 22, 52–53, 55
football, 9, 46
Fort Dearborn, 6, 16
Fox tribe, 15
freight, 39
Galena & Chicago Union Railroad, 18
gangsters, 30

gardens, 8, 54, 56
garment industry, 23
glaciers, 11, 13
Grant Park, 54
Great Chicago Fire (1871), 6, 24–25, 26, 28, 36, 43
Great Lakes, 11, 12, 16, 17, 21
Great Migration, 22, 32, 35
Greektown, 34
Green City Market, 52
Guy, Buddy, 58

HIJ

Harold Washington Library, 62
Haymarket riot (1886), 27
Heinz, 29
Hemingway, Ernest, 58
hockey, 46, 47
Home Insurance Building, 36
hot dogs, 29, 52, 53, 62
Hudson, Jennifer, 58
Hull, Bobby, 59
Hull House, 26
Humboldt Park, 34
Ice Age, 10–11, 13
ice cream, 53
Illinois and Michigan (I & M) Canal, 6, 13, 21
Illinois River, 13, 21
immigrants, 23
industry, 22–23
Jackson, Jesse, 59
Jackson Park, 28
jazz, 7, 32–33
Joliet, Louis, 16
Jordan, Michael, 47, 59

KL

Keokuk, Chief, 14
King, Martin Luther, Jr., 31
"L," 26, 39, 43
La Salle, Robert Cavelier de, 17
Lake Shore Drive, 38
lakes, 12–13, 20
Lincoln, Abraham, 30, 51
Lincoln Park, 52
Lincoln Park Zoo, 8

Little Italy, 34
Lollapalooza, 54
Loop, 9, 13, 19

MNO

Mac, Bernie, 58
Mackinac Island, 47
mammoths, 10
maps, 6, 9
Marquette, Jacques, 16
mastodons, 10
Maxwell Street Polish, 52
mayors, 31
McCormick, Cyrus, 23
meatpacking industry, 7, 22
media, 50–51
Miami tribe, 15
Michigan, Lake, 6, 8, 9, 11, 12–13, 38, 47
Midway Airport, 39
Millennium Park, 8, 38
missionaries, 16
Mississippi River, 12, 16, 17, 21
Moore, Henry, 44
Morton, Jelly Roll, 32, 33
motto, 6
movies, 51
multicultural Chicago, 34–35
murals, 34
Murray, Bill, 58
Museum Campus, 42
Museum of Science and Industry, 43
museums, 8, 34, 42–43, 54
music, 7, 32–33, 54, 58
Native Americans, 14–15, 16, 17, 62
Navy Pier, 9
neighborhoods, 8, 9, 19, 34–35, 55
newspapers, 50, 51
North Side, 6, 8, 35, 39, 46
Oak Street Beach, 54
Obama, Barack and Michelle, 59
O'Hare Airport, 39
Ojibwa tribe, 15
O'Leary, Catherine, 24
Oliver, Joe "King," 32, 33
Oriental Institute Museum, 44

Original Dixieland Jazz Band, 32
Original Rainbow Cone, 53

PQR

Palmer, Potter, 25
Palmer House Hotel, 25
parks, 8, 54, 56
Peyton, Walter, 59
Pilsen, 34
Pioneer, 18–19, 43
pizza, 52, 53
politics, 30–31, 59
population, 7
posters, 19, 22
Potawatomi tribe, 15
prairies, 11
Prohibition, 30
Puerto Rican Passage, 34
Pullman neighborhood, 19
Puppet Bike, 49
Quaker Oats, 23, 29
Race to Mackinac, 9, 47
radio stations, 50
railroads, 18–19, 39
recycling, 56
Regenstein Library, 44
Reliance Building, 36
Republican Party, 30
riots, 27, 30
River North Dance Chicago, 49
rivers, 12–13, 20
Robie House, 27
Rockefeller, John D., 44
rooftop gardens, 8, 56
Route 66, 7, 62

STUV

sailboat races 9, 47
St. Valentine's Day Massacre, 30
sand dunes, 13
Sandburg, Carl, 22
Sanitary and Ship Canal, 21
Sauk tribe, 14, 15, 17
Sears, Roebuck & Company, 26
The Second City, 48
settlers, 14, 16

sewers, 20, 21
Shedd Aquarium, 8, 42
shipping, 20–21
Silverstein, Shel, 58
skyscrapers, 7, 8, 13, 27, 36–37, 54
Smart Museum of Art, 45
South Side, 6, 8, 34, 35, 39, 44, 46, 53
sports, 9, 46–47, 59
Starr, Ellen Gates, 26
Steppenwolf Theatre Company, 48
street festivals, 55
streetcars, 22
sweatshops, 23
television stations, 50
Terkel, Studs, 58
theaters, 48–49
transportation, 7, 18–19, 20–21, 22, 38–39
Tribune Company, 50
Tribune Tower, 51
Trump Tower, 37
tunnels, 21, 39
Tweedy, Jeff, 58
Union Station, 18
Union Stockyards, 22
University of Chicago, 44–45

WXYZ

Washington, Harold, 31
water supply, 21, 25
waterways, 20–21
Weissmuller, Johnny, 58
Wells, Ida B., 28
West Side, 6, 8
White Sox, 9, 46
Willis Tower, 8, 37, 62
"Windy City," 7, 62
Winfrey, Oprah, 50, 58
Winnebago tribe, 14
World's Fair (1893), 6, 28–29, 62
Wright, Frank Lloyd, 27, 45
zoos, 8

Acknowledgments

Pearson Education wishes to thank Chicago Public Schools and Waukegan School District 60, as well as the following teachers, for their reviews of this book and for the creation of supplemental educational materials:

Chicago, IL: **Jada Gilleylen**, Sutherland Elementary School; **Adam Geisler**, Bateman Elementary School. Waukegan, IL: **Nancy Johnson**, Greenwood Elementary School; **Diana Plunkett**, Glenwood Elementary School; **Susanna Pries**, Washington Elementary School.

The publisher would like to thank the following for their kind permission to reproduce their photographs:

(Key: a-above; b-below/bottom; c-center; f-far; l-left; r-right; t-top)

4 Dorling Kindersley: The Field Museum, Chicago (bl); HMV / EMI Records (cla). **6 Getty Images:** Raymond Boyd / Michael Ochs Archives (tl). **7 Corbis:** Bettmann (tl, tr). **8 Dorling Kindersley:** John G. Shedd Aquarium (bl). **9 Corbis:** Joseph Sohm / Visions of America (bl). **10 Corbis:** National Geographic Society (tl). **11 Corbis:** Ashley Cooper (tl); David Muench (tr). **12 NASA:** JPL (tr). **13 Corbis:** David Frazier (bl); David Muench (cl); José Fuste Raga (br). **14 Dorling Kindersley:** American Museum of Natural History (clb). **Mary Evans Picture Library:** (r). **15 Dorling Kindersley:** American Museum of Natural History

(l, tr, ca, br). **16 Corbis:** Bettmann (t, cra). **16-17 Getty Images:** Chicago History Museum (b). **17 Alamy Images:** North Wind Picture Archives (tr). **Corbis:** Bettmann (tl). **Getty Images:** Chicago History Museum (ca). **18 Corbis:** Lake County Museum (tr). **18-19 Chicago History Museum:** Kaufman & Fabry, negative no. IChi-37010 (main image). **19 Getty Images:** Andreas Feininger / Time & Life Pictures (crb); MPI (tr). **20 Corbis:** Bettmann (tl). **SuperStock:** Visions of America / Purestock (bl). **21 Corbis:** Willard Culver / National Geographic Society (br). **Getty Images:** Chicago History Museum (cla, tr); Field Museum Library (cr). **22 Corbis:** Historical Picture Archive (bl). **Getty Images:** Chicago History Museum (br); MPI (cra). **23 Chicago History Museum:** negative no. DN-0002416 (t). **Corbis:** Bettmann (bl). **Getty Images:** Transcendental Graphics (crb). **24 Alamy Images:** North Wind Picture Archives (b). **Corbis:** Bettmann (tr). **25 Corbis:** Bettmann (tr). **Getty Images:** Lake County Museum / Curt Teich Postcard Archives (br); Three Lions / Hulton Archive (tl). **26 Corbis:** Bettmann (bl). **26-27 Getty Images:** Hulton Archive (main image). **27 Corbis:** Richard Bryant / Arcaid (bl). **Getty Images:** Tim Boyle (br). **28 Corbis:** Bettmann (cl). **Getty Images:** Chicago History Museum (tr). **28-29 Corbis:** Bettmann (b). **29 Corbis:** Bettmann (tl). **Courtesy H. J. Heinz Company Limited:** (br). **Mary Evans Picture Library:** (cra). **30 Alamy Images:** Lordprice Collection (tl). **Corbis:** Bettmann (b). **Getty Images:** PhotoQuest (cra). **31 Corbis:** Bettmann (tl, tr). **Getty Images:** Julian Wasser /

Time & Life Pictures (main image). **32 Dorling Kindersley:** Courtesy of Sony Music Entertainment (tl). **Getty Images:** Frank Driggs Collection (b). **33 Corbis:** Bettmann; (tr, ca). **Dorling Kindersley:** HMV / EMI Records (bl). **34 Getty Images:** Eliezer Appleton / Flickr (cla). **35 Corbis:** Brittany Somerset (br). **Library Of Congress, Washington, D.C.:** (tl). **36-37 Corbis:** Radius Images (b). **36 Getty Images:** Chicago History Museum (cla). **37 Corbis:** Bob Krist (tr). **38 Corbis:** Adam Jones / Visuals Unlimited (b); Don Mason / Blend Images (tr). **39 Getty Images:** Karen Bleier / AFP (br); (c). **40 Corbis:** Lake County Museum (tr). **Getty Images:** Tim Boyle / Bloomberg (bl). **41 Alamy Images:** Wildgruber / F1online digitale Bildagentur GmbH (r). **Corbis:** John Gress / Reuters (clb). **Courtesy of the Early Office Museum (www.officemuseum.com):** (tl). **42 Alamy Images:** Kim Karpeles (b). **Dorling Kindersley:** Adler Planetarium & Astronomy Museum (cl). **42-43 Corbis:** John Weinstein, The Field Museum / Reuters (main image). **43 Corbis:** Franz-Marc Frei (tr). **Dorling Kindersley:** Museum of Science and Industry, Chicago, Il (tl). **44 Dorling Kindersley:** The work illustrated ("Nuclear Energy") is reproduced by permission of the Henry Moore Foundation (tl); Oriental Institute Museum (ca). **45 Dorling Kindersley:** Bond Chapel, Chicago (clb, bl). **46 Corbis:** Robin Alam / Icon SMI (bl). **Getty Images:** Jonathan Daniel (tl). **47 Corbis:** Steve Lipofsky (bc); Tannen Maury / EPA (r). **Getty Images:** Jeff Haynes / AFP (clb); Jim Prisching (tl). **48 Flickr.com:** Mike Lee (mikeleeorg) (bl).

48-49 River North Dance Chicago: photo by Cheryl Mann (dancers). **49 Getty Images:** Nicholas Markos / Flickr (ca). **50 Alamy Images:** Christopher Purcell (tl). **Corbis:** Walter McBride / Retna Ltd. (tr); Katy Winn (br). **50-51 Dorling Kindersley:** The Tribune Company (main image). **51 Alamy Images:** Warner Bros / AF archive (bl). **52 Alamy Images:** Sarah Hadley (b). **Getty Images:** Joel Richardson / The Washington Post (tr). **53 Dreamstime.com:** Cafebeanz Company (cl). **Original Rainbow Cone:** (tr). **Joe Viesti / viestiphoto.com:** (tl). **54 Alamy Images:** Chuck Eckert (b). **Corbis:** Rob Grabowski / Retna Ltd. (cla). **55 Alamy Images:** Chuck Eckert (tr). **Corbis:** John Gress / Reuters (main image). **56 Corbis:** Art on File (cr). **Getty Images:** Tim Boyle (tl); Amanda Hall / Robert Harding World Imagery (tr). **57 Corbis:** LuckyPix. **58 Getty Images:** Tim Mosenfelder (br); Ron Sachs / CNP (bl). **59 Corbis:** Gary Gardiner / EPA (r). **Getty Images:** Melchior DiGiacomo (tr). **61 Corbis:** Joseph Sohm / Visions of America (tl); John Weinstein, The Field Museum / Reuters (cb).

Jacket images: Front: **Corbis:** Ed Boettcher b, Joshua Roberts / Pool tc; **Dorling Kindersley:** The work illustrated ("Nuclear Energy") is reproduced by permission of the Henry Moore Foundation tl/ (sculpture).

All other images © Dorling Kindersley
For further information see:
www.dkimages.com